Natures Inspirations

Natures Inspirations

A collection of original and uplifting
messages in poetry

Barbara Martin

Copyright 2013 Barbara Martin

All rights reserved. This book, or any parts thereof,
may not be reproduced in any form without
permission from the publisher

ISBN:978-0-615-63115-8

All photos by Barbara Martin
in Wentworth New Hampshire

A walk in nature surrounds us
with inspiring messages

All we need to do is listen...

Believe

Believe in things you cannot see
believe in dreams yet to be
let your heart bring it all true
for no one else can dream like you

Do not listen to things that are not
and spend no time when others ought
yet hear that which is deep inside
for your dreams should never hide

Time knows how much time it has
no need to hurry I know this as
my life moves on so slowly still
to be at peace I know I will

Believe that all awaits you yet
in hopes and dreams and those you've met
and know your dreams will come true
when you believe they're all in you

Footprints

I've chosen my path to take
leaving footprints you can see
but you have your own to make
to leave your legacy

If you were to follow me
you wouldn't leave your own
imagine how that would be
not learning on your own

I would be so proud of you
to know that what you'll earn
with each forward step you take
you will value what you learn

Different

I used to wonder why I was
so different from the rest
but now I know it is because
to be unique is to be blessed

My purpose hides so simply here
I need not look away
life's reasons are so very clear
to treasure love today

And worry not what others do
or judge me for my being
for is it not they're different too
the truth they are not seeing

So find your reason and live it
despite weeds in the way
to simply love makes purpose fit
and your heart always obey

Just a Leaf

Please notice me
before I'm gone
my brilliant beauty
won't last long

My colors are bold
against the sky
quite gorgeous I'm told
before I die

Tell me not
a sad goodbye
my fate to rot
don't question why

No tears for me
spare me your grief
because you see
I'm just a leaf

Judgment

Safety in numbers they find me
looming tall in their menacing way
casting judgment so cruel and freely
as if it's just part of their day

They find me alone yet fearless
for the wind of truth will come
it will tear their long trunks into pieces
their mock bravery over and done

As cowards they'll splinter and falter
their true selves now shattered and bare
to have seen such behavior so altered
I will tell you I don't really care

Live in the Moment

Your glorious cascade
spills beauty into motion
a rushing serenade
fills me with deep emotion

I know not where you've been
or where it is you're going
Do you worry now and then
with feelings you're not showing

Your wisdom now I see
although I'm not sure how
is what you just taught me
is simply to live for now

Intimidation

Someone next to you may not agree
with your choice of direction
be true to yourself and simply be
immune to their reflection

Their efforts to control you
will be futile if you choose
their weaknesses to see through
and they will always lose

Continue on just as you do
while they will stay the same
this worked with someone that I knew
but I'll never share his name

Fear

What name have you from whom I hide
your powers upon me grace
failing to escape each time I've tried
your reflection is on my face

Why must you haunt me following so
my life despite my dreams
what will it take to let you go
is it easier than what it seems

Meanwhile my dreams pass me by
my talents yet not spoken
to believe in myself and to try
your spell would then be broken

No longer will I hide from you
your name no longer near
I realize what I always knew
now gone your name was fear

Look to the Mountain

The years pass by as you become old
with choices you've made only you hold
a mountain before you yet a different kind
for the mountain before you is all in your mind

Your journey is before you whatever the cost
to find peace and no longer be lost
your mountain awaits you in time yet to come
with true love and happiness before life is done

And so with these words from my heart I do write
may all the wrongs in your life become right
and wish one day there will be a tomorrow
when your spirit flies free from all of your sorrow

For on that day you will search no more
and your life will be as never before
for on that day when you finally succeed
you'll find you always had all that you need

Letting Go

(There may be a time when
it's best to just let go)

How weary it's been
to hold the weight
of this burden
pulling on me

I now let you go
and leave to fate
my choice
to set myself free

Where you should fall
it's not my place
to worry
or carry you any longer

so now we depart
and with you I replace
for my freedom
I now can grow stronger

Forgiveness

Forgiveness found its way to me
through the darkness of my pain
with consuming anger yet now I see
I shall never again be the same

This warming gift of letting go
my choice to cease to hate
it revealed itself for me to know
to forgive is never too late

Why did it take so many years
if it was waiting all the time
it matters not for now I see
the choice was always mine

The brightest of forgiving love
has captured me now forever
a treasured message from above
for to hate will now be never

Simple Joy

Warm sun invites me
words I cannot say
so soft a breeze I cannot see
God gave me this beautiful day

How lucky I was this morning
to be alive and to be here
to some my life is boring
for me a day so dear

My joy comes from simple things
I need not have too many
for if I was given too much money
I'd rather not have any

I know not how long my life will be
God has that in his plan
I have today and I have me
and what I can do I can

Chasing a Rainbow

How often we look so far away
for what we think we're missing
unable to see in our dismay
to ourselves we are not listening

Trying to grasp beyond our reach
convinced it's all so far
perhaps this rainbow is trying to teach
it's all where we already are

The end of this rainbow is right here
and its message is clear to see
it tells me what I need to hear
for right here is where I should be

Good Morning Sun

Good morning sun
where have you been
your happiness greets me
and warms me within

If you are my gift
than what can I do
for what you give me
I cannot give you

So freely you offer
your warm embrace
the light from your soul
is a kiss on my face

I thank you for knowing
that where ever I'll be
for the rest of my life
you'll be following me

Celebrate Life

Was it by chance I grew here
or was it meant to be
with my glorious colors I live near
in memory of you as a tree

I celebrate the life you once had
as proud as any friend can show
my blossoms smile that I'm so glad
it was you I was able to know

I will not be choosing sorrow
to spend the rest of my time
for it could very well be tomorrow
the last day of life is mine

Until then I'll treasure the suns kiss
the warmth of its rays on my leaves
and not grieve over those whom I do miss
because the future nobody sees

Loss Brings Growth

If ever someone comes along
and robs you of what they lack
be like me and be strong
for you can grow it back

The pain of loss can be great
a missing part of you
hold your ground and simply wait
as time brings life anew

Always reach up and never down
look up to the sun to grow
learn from what you've left on the ground
and share for others to know

Reflections of a Life

Friend or foe who might you be
peering back in my direction
I treasure so your honesty
since you are my own reflection

May I ask you if I could
for you know myself so well
has my life been all it should
I need for you to tell

Has my purpose been fulfilled
my destiny home to rest
with faith in God firmly instilled
letting go of all the rest

Before my life finds its end
I know one thing is true
for these answers I can depend
I will find them all in you

The Road Home

The road before me calls my name
inviting me to follow
promising I won't be the same
if I leave behind my sorrow

And to worry not with loss or grief
but let joy carry away my tears
through love I shall always find relief
and strength to release my fears

Let love always be your daily guide
and know that only time knows when
the love that keeps us eternally tied
shall bring us together again

And should you ever feel all alone
or feel lost for what to do
remember love grows where its seeds are sown
and the way home is waiting for you

My Point of View

How many times
in life we see
the same sometimes
yet disagree

For what we say
can only be
a truth to weigh
to some degree

Perhaps we all
can't see the same
if we recall
our pasts to blame

So if you trust
my words to you
they're simply just
my point of view

Self Respect and Dignity

Self respect and dignity
came to me one day
I didn't recognize them
and knew not what to say

They both began to ask me
if I would let them show
how they could truly offer
themselves for me to know

I then began to listen
and heard promise in their voice
I knew that I was given
the power of my choice

I suddenly felt stronger
together with them now
powerless I am no longer
their wisdom taught me how

Understanding

I sat upon a bench one day
that faced the open sea
and thought I heard not far away
a voice that said to me

Your past which is behind you now
awaits for you to find
the lessons that will show you how
our lives are all entwined

For those who brought you grief and pain
a gift to you they're sending
let there be no fault or blame
but only understanding

And like the stone tossed into the sea
that leaves behind its wave
you've touched others for what can be
the lessons that you gave

Follow Your Dream

There lives a dream in each of us
that waits for us to find
our own unique and true purpose
to which we may be blind

Yet just because we cannot see
does not mean it's not real
for when we know a thing can be
our dream can be revealed

And let not others disapprove
of what you know can be
they have no power to remove
the dream that you can see

So as your dream begins to rise
reflecting what you feel
no longer lost nor in disguise
your dream shall now be real

Solitude

There are times when we
need to find a place
to resolve to see
what we choose to face

And to be alone
may be what's best to do
for only we own
what we decide to do

The silence will say
when patience draws near
to then show the way
what you need to hear

And soon you shall find
what solitude brings
is clearness to mind
to count your blessings

Be Your True Color

A modest flower spoke to me
its color bright and clear
of how perhaps it came to be
what it wanted me to hear

It knew that I had lost my way
not knowing who I was
and so to me it then did say
you are confused because

The time you take to look outside
to others for your soul
then you will truly be denied
that which can make you whole

For what you truly cannot see
your heart will always call
to find in such simplicity
you were never lost at all

My Garden

My garden greets me every day
a gift for me to see
such brilliant beauty on display
alive here just for me

It needs my care and tending to
for it to grow and bloom
but if my work is overdue
there may be little room

For in among the planted seeds
as they began to grow
came uninvited nasty weeds
I didn't want to know

With selfish aim they crept and crawled
to not let beauty live
their purpose was to ruin all
my garden had to give

I knew then what I had to do
and tore them from the ground
my garden given life anew
with freedom finally found

Stone Wall

Who built this wall around your heart
why is it hard and cold
your wall is what keeps us apart
and now you're frail and old

How many years has it taken
for you to place each stone
so many others you've forsaken
and now you're all alone

Throughout my life I've tried to take
each stone down one by one
I truly wanted you to make
your life a happy one

But now I see it can't be so
your wall is strong and true
I only wish for you to know
I always have loved you

Above the Fog

Years ago I couldn't see
trying to find my way
I didn't know who to be
or what I should say

I tried to be what others said
of how I should fit in
but now I know I was misled
from what I've learned since then

Unhappiness drove me away
to find where I belong
and now to you I can truly say
I know now they were wrong

For others should not ever tell
someone how to be
I know now so very well
when above the fog I found me

Distractions

Annoying so they crowd me
and linger in my way
relentlessly they beg and plea
to make me look away

They simply want attention
and yearn to waste my time
they tempt me with pretension
that their values are mine

But if I keep my vision
and focus on my goal
they can't change my decision
to take back what they stole

And so I will not falter
for I learned something new
distractions will not alter
whatever I want to do

New Beginnings

An ending doesn't always mean
that all is lost forever
to look beyond what it may seem
can bring a new endeavor

If we hold our past and dwell
we can't be free to grow
with love we can bid it farewell
for it taught us all we know

Some endings can bring sorrow
I know too well that's true
but today will bring tomorrow
with a new beginning for you

Determination

Have you ever struggled with
a problem on your own
and others choose not to give
help when you're all alone

It seems like they don't even care
if you succeed or not
and stand by to calmly stare
at you so distraught

Determination is your friend
trust it will never fail
to bring success in the end
whatever it entails

And when you do you shall find
that when you have succeeded
wiser now then you won't mind
their help you never needed

Seeds of an Idea

They eagerly anticipate
the time when they will dare
to follow faith and dissipate
their journey through the air

Surrendered to the winds of fate
each seed can bring alive
no longer holding back to wait
its idea to grow and thrive

How quickly some may disapprove
tell them to then take heed
for your idea may one day prove
that it's not just a weed

Hate

What is it that you've learned so well
so frozen is your soul
that just by looking I can tell
your heart is half not whole

What is missing that you must
choose hate with cold distain
I fear the answer is I trust
that you find fault and blame

But what do others have to do
with how you choose to feel
you might consider something new
and make a choice to heal

To melt away your frozen hate
will show what's truly there
please know this before it's too late
you can if you truly care

Life is Full Circle

Each beginning has an end
my buds will bloom with grace
my gift for you I hope to send
a smile upon your face

To be treasured like a love
that visits for a time
at least for now I can dream of
the love I wish was mine

Yet knowing all the while one day
the wind will come to send
my blossoms all so far away
but one day I'll have more again

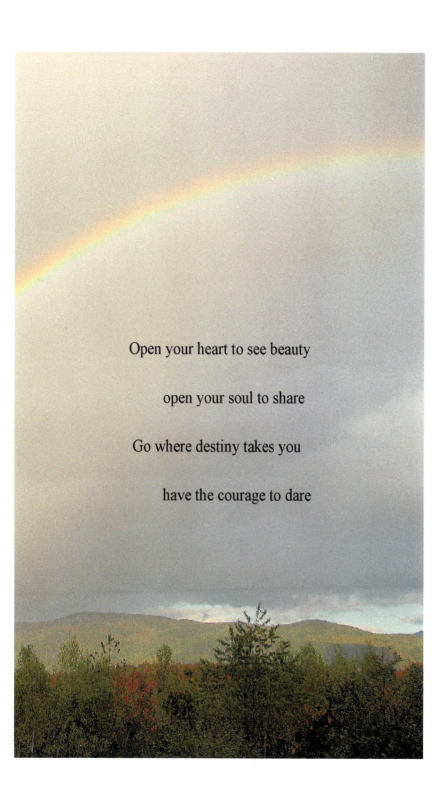

Open your heart to see beauty

open your soul to share

Go where destiny takes you

have the courage to dare